The Mediterranean Cat

Hans Silvester

CHRONICLE BOOKS

SAN FRANCISCO

First published in the United States in 1996 by Chronicle Books

Copyright © 1995 by Editions de la Martinière

Translation copyright © 1996 by Chronicle Books

Jacket design by Lucy Nielsen

Library of Congress Cataloging-in-Publication Data available

ISBN 0-8118-2096-3

Printed in France

Distributed in Canada by Raincoast Books
8680 Cambie Street
Vancouver, B.C. V6P 6M9

10 9 8 7 6 5 4 3 2 1

Chronicle Books
85 Second Street
San Francisco, California 94105

Web Site: www.chronbooks.com

The Mediterranean Cat

HANS SILVESTER

To live happily, a cat needs several things: something to eat and drink, shelter and a quiet place to sleep, a sandy corner for the call of nature, and above all, the love of a human being. This is the bare minimum.

But to be truly happy, a cat requires much more: a personal territory to satisfy the hunting instinct, a place to meet other cats, a playmate, a tree to climb and claw, and a varied diet. Many cats lack these elements, but what today's cat most sorely lacks is a communal life, a relationship with other cats.

My observations of undomesticated cats in Greece showed me that they choose a tribal way of living, one that permits the individual to be with others or to be alone, according to the desire of the moment. This behavior resembles that of humans.

The typical tribal group is enlivened by an old female cat—the true leader of the clan who is always ready to defend her own against all aggressors. She has the best knowledge of the territory and is usually the one who brings back living prey to teach the youngsters to hunt. Often, she and her daughters suckle and raise their little ones as a committee. Within the group, several males can coexist without trouble, but it seems that there is always a dominant male who is well respected by the others. This cat gets along extremely well with the old dominant female, who is probably his mother. These two are easily recognized by their bearing and their distinctive character. In the various neighborhoods, they are the favorites of the people who care for the cats. On the Greek isles cats have no appointed owner and live entirely outdoors.

In the limited space of a little island village, the male and female cats know each other very well. They recognize each other from a distance and avoid or seek out certain meetings, thus simplifying relations. For a friendly greeting they rub noses, one cat's tail encircling the body of the other. Males and females defend their territory—it's the only cause of the veritable brawls that often result in grave wounds. The male cat changes considerably between birth and adulthood—the adorable little kit transforms into a big, stubborn tomcat. The caterwauling that is heard at night is almost always the cry of a female cat in heat who is defending herself against the males. The terrible battles for territory are waged in silence.

In my photos I try to show the richness and intensity of the family and social life of cats. Living in a social group is certainly a source of pleasure for each of them. By contrast, the solitary house cat is hardly understood by its owner. Because to truly understand a cat, it is necessary to observe it socially, in contact with other cats.

Our house in Provence is part of a little hamlet situated on a hill, on the edge of cultivated fields beyond which is scrubland. It is a place where life is good—for people and for cats. The house is very old, more than three centuries old. Many generations

have lived there, along with an incalculable number of cats. Cats love old houses and the old trees nearby. At our house they love the interior courtyard with its old fig tree and trellis. The number of inhabitants in this hamlet has greatly diminished—of sixteen households of olden days, only four families remain, each with its cats. Most of the domestic animals who brought life to the hamlet, such as sheep, goats, donkeys, horses, and rabbits, have disappeared; only two dogs, some cats, hens, and doves have survived. Among these the cat is unique, being at once the most independent and the most attached to the hearth.

For the last thirty-five years cats have shared our house, enriched our lives, brought us happiness. Deprived of cats, a house in the country is a sad house, lacking an essential element of life. It is a home that becomes prey to mice and rats. The country folk understand this—there is at least one cat per farm.

You quickly become used to the presence of a cat. In a short time a cat finds his place in the life of the household. You do not own a cat—in truth, you share your life with him. In the most natural way he becomes co-owner of the house and its surroundings. A cat needs to feel like a full-fledged member of the family.

Another point: we have never made our cats work. In fact, we have never managed to train any of them. They have never supplied us with anything—we do not eat their flesh. Nevertheless, cats do provide one great service: they hunt mice and rats, which in the past have spread the most dreadful epidemics. But the presence of cats throughout the world is due principally to their charm and grace, and to the physical pleasure we receive when caressing them.

If he so wishes, our cat can stay in the house all day, but according to the custom of Provençal country folk, we send him out at night on a mouse-hunting mission. In the morning he waits at the front door and joins us for breakfast. Regretfully, he can't tell us the story of his nighttime roving, but we are free to imagine his adventures. It's certain he hasn't slept much. He is much more tired in the morning than in the evening. Upon his return, he grooms by licking himself, wiping away the traces of the night's experiences before relaxing completely and sleeping. It's truly a double life—the day is spent with people, but at night it's the wild life of the feline. If the cat doesn't return in the morning, we feel a disagreeable absence in the house.

Our cats are and always have been very discreet about their private lives, about what they do at night, in secret places. Even in the country, with a cat who is entirely free in his movements, one only sees him alone—he jealously guards the mystery of his meetings. In order to explain why I have devoted so many years of attention and patience to observing cats in Greece, I would like to introduce to you the cats who have lived with us in Provence. They are the ones who have led me to better understand the complexity of the cat, to become deeply interested in its behavior.

In 1961, a friend gave us our first cat, Peter, a spotted black-and-white who lived more than ten years with us. I especially remember his coming back to the house, seriously wounded in the course of terrible brawls, asking to be cared for so he could head off as soon as possible for new adventures.

After Peter came Francisco, who lived alongside us for eighteen years. The folks who gave us the cat said Francisco was a male and so we believed until the day when the truth burst out from her very round belly! Three times she had kittens, which we raised and then gave to neighbors. Francisco lived with us when our daughter was born, and she always showed the greatest understanding to the baby, willingly allowing herself to become a toy—it was never the least problem. A child learns much from being around a cat, above all that there are limits that must not be crossed; once crossed, the cat defends itself or leaves. At our house, a true friendship was born between the little girl and the animal.

This tabby cat, Francisco, was a remarkable hunter. Over the course of her life she must have brought hundreds and hundreds of field mice into our courtyard to devour them. Curiously, she was not interested in the house mice; for her, they were not fair game. We had to catch them with traps since she let them escape inside the house. This cat was very independent—we were the only ones allowed to pet her. Francisco reached the age of eighteen years—exceptional for a cat living in the country—and died a gentle, peaceful death from old age. We buried her at the edge of the vegetable garden.

Our next cat, Greco, was a proud reddish-brown tabby. I had found him in Greece when he was a tiny kitten half-dead of hunger. He shared the first year of his life with us, but quickly became very curious and fiercely independent. His territory grew progressively wider. We worried about him, especially when we caught sight of foxes in our car headlights when returning home late at night. But in Provence there is something more dangerous than foxes—hunters. Not only do hunters set out poison for foxes, which claims many cats and dogs as victims, but because there is so little game, some use country cats for target practice, even in close proximity to farms and hamlets.

One fine day Greco disappeared. We looked for him in the village and in the countryside, but in vain. There was not the least trace of him. He left a great emptiness, and we missed him very much. Greco was no ordinary cat—he had managed to become a true friend.

With Greco gone we decided to go to the Society for the Protection of Animals in the hopes of finding a kitten. At first they showed us grown cats locked in a cage. It was such a sad image—the worried look, the dull fur. Then we saw two kittens kept in a bird cage. Seeing us, they climbed like monkeys, clinging to the grillwork, showing us their pretty bellies. One of the kittens was black and white, the other a tabby; we decided immediately on the tabby, a little female. A half-hour later she was exploring our interior courtyard. We called her Hydra, after the Greek island that Greco came from.

She had a particular talent for climbing and quickly found herself some perfectly safe nestling places on the windowsills reached by the branches of the fig tree. Hydra saw without being seen. She had an innate sense of the hunt—by far her favorite game. She amused herself with all sorts of insects, getting herself stung regularly by wasps and bees. Hydra caught her first mice at a young age; at six months she brought back her first rat, which was almost as big as she was. She came immediately when we called her, happy to have the attention, rolling onto her back and purring with happiness. She was extremely sweet and gentle, full of trust in us, in everyone. The interior courtyard, which she preferred over the house, was her kingdom. In summer, our courtyard became our sitting room, and she was delighted to be so close to us and to share our life fully.

That year we left for Greece in mid-September, entrusting the house to our daughter and her boyfriend. During a phone conversation we learned that Hydra had disappeared, like Greco, in autumn, in the fox hunting season. At the time we were on the island of Hydra once again and quickly decided to bring back one of these little kittens born in the fall, who have little chance of surviving through the winter. In fact, many people leave the island during the winter season—the fishermen leave to escape the bad weather—so the cats have less food and many kittens do not survive very long. In the island's little port we found a gray and white kitten under an old abandoned boat. I was surely the first human to touch him. Hardly bigger than my hand, he defended himself like a little devil. He became our Greco II. At first, in the hotel, he was wild and very afraid, but from the third day on, he accepted us. He bravely boarded the Athens-Marseilles flight—as a stowaway.

Greco II is the first cat I can reproach for being egotistical. He has succeeded in getting into all the

houses in the hamlet and has been made welcome in each. A neighbor who does not care much for cats even calls him "Monsieur Greco." This cat has a strong personality and feels very sure of himself in all situations, always giving the impression of calmness and strength. At home, he allows himself to be petted, but when out-of-doors he's the one who decides whether or not he will come near.

He takes great care with his grooming and is always impeccable. He does not bite or scratch, but if something bothers him, he clearly shows that he is a force to be reckoned with, ready to use his claws and teeth. Greco II takes himself very seriously and obviously feels he is a very important cat, and he shows it every chance he gets. He expects to be in charge. His exceptional beauty enhances his authority—he has a light gray coat with white paws, a pink nose, and green eyes. In the house, his favorite spot is in the armchair in front of the fireplace.

Each year, in winter, the heavens bestow upon us days that are better spent inside near the fireplace. This is the season of the violent mistral, the cold winds that buffet southern France, when snow falls in the north. We are convinced that the roof tiles will blow away and fear the heater is going to give up the struggle. The cats feel this harsh weather coming long ahead of time. They refuse then to leave the house. Greco plays dead in front of the fire, covering his eyes with his paws so he won't see or hear the tempest. He can spend an entire day this way. But he is not really sleeping, only waiting for the return of fine weather.

Our daughter is Greco's great friend. When she comes to the house, he hurries over to be petted. He sucks the fabric of her blouse or sweater, imitating with his paws the movements of a kitten suckling his mother. He purrs very loudly—this is for him the summit of well-being.

Greco is very playful. If he catches sight of another cat he tries to draw him into a game. They run across the village square, shoot up an almond tree at full speed, leap onto a roof, the race continuing all over the hamlet. When the two cats grow tired they will commence a play-fight, nipping and clawing without trying to hurt one another. Little by little the game grows more intense—some fur flies, the fighters begin to hurt each other, they yowl. Suddenly the game halts and each cat leaves the scene without looking at the other.

Greco is a mediocre hunter, but he is proud to arrive home with a living catch between his teeth.

He must be congratulated before he will begin to eat his victim. He leaves no scraps—sparrows disappear with all their feathers. His natural authority is fully respected by the other cats in the hamlet. Even before stray dogs he makes his presence known, always ready to attack, never to flee. He doesn't spend that much time with us, only a few hours a day. Greco has lived with us for two years now, and his behavior always surprises us. He is certainly the most interesting cat who has lived in our house, and his presence means much to us.

For a short time now we have also had a female cat in our household, inherited from an aged neighbor who was obliged to return to the United States because of poor health. It was very hard for her to leave without her beloved Kitty, a tabby with black stripes on her flanks, but taking the cat to a retirement home was out of the question. She departed after leaving a few days' worth of food in her garden. Feeling guilty about abandoning her cat, she had not asked us to take care of Kitty. The cat, for her part, had felt long before her owner's departure that her life was going to change. All cats are endowed with the gift of sensing important changes before they occur. Even before she was hungry she came directly to our house. In a few hours, Kitty had realized that we were her future. Greco doesn't like her very much, but he tolerates her, always taking care to show her that he is the boss.

Every cat who has lived with us has had a very distinctive personality, a pronounced individuality. All have been very independent yet, at the same time, very affectionate. It is clear that there are as many differences between cats as there are between people.

There is an island in the Cyclades, west of Greece in the Aegean Sea, where there are more cats than people. The inhabitants are fishermen and peasants. On this island there are only two little grocery stores and a café—Kafénéion—that is open year-round. Visitors will find a few rooms for rent in people's homes but no hotel. The ferry docks two times a week, and only in calm weather. (I won't give away the name of the island; its balance is very fragile, and I don't wish to see it overrun with tourists.)

There are paths cut out for donkeys but no roads, so no cars. In the houses, however, there is running water, electricity, and television. Everyone knows one another and the men like to chat in the café; it's easier to find a priest in the café than in the church. Life has always been difficult on this island, and it still is. To those who work very hard, the earth and sea provide enough to live on simply, but it is almost impossible to earn money. The young people have little choice but to leave the island to work on boats or in Athens or even to emigrate to the United States in order to earn at least enough to marry and build a house. So the young men have traveled, have known a different life, have learned English, and, to maintain a balance: the weakest animals die. The growth of the feline population is such that either man or nature must stabilize their number.

I have observed the cats of the Greek isles for quite some time and I have come to know them well—they recognized me each time that I returned. Each time I have seen the same happy harmony between inhabitants, strangers, and cats. As it is a minuscule world, it is easy for an outside observer to find himself at the heart of these intersecting lives. Observing is enough—the village transforms into a sort of theater. The cats, of course, are the talented actors. Patience and discretion are enough to make you a witness to their behavior. Their intimate life takes place in the street—all you have to do is watch them for a while without disturbing them. Of course, I have a completely different kind of contact with our cats in Provence, who I think are happy. Those that I photographed in Greece are less spoiled, have a harder life, but live in families and in tribes—their relationship with man is a different one. They know a different happiness.

especially, have learned to evaluate the advantages and inconveniences of life on their little island.

Those who return have made the decision to live there and share life with the cats; the latter are so ubiquitous that life on the island is unbearable unless you like them. If you look out over the sea, you see cats on board the boats. If you go to the café, you are surrounded by cats. In the alleyways, in front of the houses, you find them again. The center of their lives is the port, where their source of food—fish—is found. The day's catch is eaten there by the inhabitants and by the cats who benefit from the extraordinary generosity of the fishermen. Only in winter, when the weather is bad, do the cats go hungry. In these extreme conditions nature intervenes